W9-BMH-334

$$\mathbf{G} = \frac{1}{c}\int [\mathbf{D}\cdot\mathbf{H}]\,dS$$

$$\delta g_{\mu\nu} = g_{\mu\nu}\delta\rho, \quad \delta\phi_\mu = \frac{\partial(\delta\rho)}{\partial x_\mu}$$

$$G_x = \frac{1}{c}\int (D_y H_z - D_z H_y)\,dS$$

$$\frac{d\phi}{ds} = \frac{\partial\phi}{\partial x_\mu}\frac{dx_\mu}{ds}$$

$$\mathbf{F}(\Sigma) = \left(l^2, \frac{l^2}{\beta}, \frac{l^2}{\beta}\right)\mathbf{F}(\Sigma')$$

$$\psi = \frac{\partial\phi}{dx_\mu}\frac{dx_\mu}{ds}$$

$$\frac{\partial w^\mu}{\partial x_\mu} \equiv \mathfrak{W}^\mu_\mu$$

$$\frac{\partial\mathfrak{W}^\mu_\nu}{\partial x_\mu} - \Gamma^\alpha_{\nu\beta}\mathfrak{W}^\beta_\alpha \equiv \tfrac{1}{2}F$$

$$\frac{\beta(r'_0 - r')}{lc} = \beta^2\frac{v\xi}{c^2} + \frac{\beta}{lc}\left(\xi\frac{\partial r'}{\partial x} + \eta\frac{\partial r'}{\partial y} + \zeta\frac{\partial r'}{\partial z}\right)$$

$$A_\mu = \frac{\partial\phi}{\partial x_\mu}$$

$$\frac{\gamma_{\mu\nu}}{2} = 2\kappa T^*_{\mu\nu}$$

$$P_x = \int\rho\xi\,dS, \quad P_y = \int\rho\eta\,dS, \quad P_z = \int\rho\zeta\,dS$$

$$\begin{bmatrix}\mu\nu\\\alpha\end{bmatrix} = g_{\alpha\beta}\Gamma^\beta_{\mu\nu}$$

$$\frac{dP_x}{dt} = \int\rho u_x\,dS, \quad \frac{dP_y}{dt} = \int\rho u_y\,dS, \quad \frac{dP_z}{dt} = \int\rho u_z\,d$$

$$u_\xi = \frac{u_x - v}{1 - u_x v/c^2}$$

$$u_\eta = \frac{u_y}{\beta(1 - u_x v/c^2)}$$

$$\int K_1\,dx_1 dx_2 dx_3 = \int \frac{\partial T_{14}}{\partial x_4}\,dx_1 dx_2 dx$$

$$u_\zeta = \frac{u_2}{\beta(1 - u_x v/c^2)},$$

$$-i\frac{d}{dt}$$

$$\begin{bmatrix}\mu\nu\\\alpha\end{bmatrix} = g_{\alpha\beta}\Gamma^\beta_{\mu\nu}$$

$$\rho' = \frac{\partial X'}{\partial\xi} + \frac{\partial Y'}{\partial\eta} + \frac{\partial Z'}{\partial\zeta}$$
$$= \beta(1 - u_x v/c^2)\rho.$$

$$\mathbf{G} = \frac{1}{c}\int[\mathbf{D}\cdot\mathbf{H}]dS$$

$$\delta g_{\mu\nu} = g_{\mu\nu}\delta\rho, \quad \delta\phi_\mu = \frac{\partial(}{\zeta}$$

$$\mathbf{G}_x = \frac{1}{c}\int(\mathbf{D}_y\mathbf{H}_z - \mathbf{D}_z\mathbf{H}_y)\,dS$$

$$\frac{d\phi}{ds} = \frac{\partial\phi}{\partial x_\mu}\frac{dx_\mu}{ds}$$

$$\mathbf{F}(\Sigma) = \left(l^2, \frac{l^2}{\beta}, \frac{l^2}{\beta}\right)\mathbf{F}$$

$$\psi = \frac{\partial\phi}{\partial x_\mu}\frac{dx_\mu}{ds}$$

$$\frac{\partial\mathfrak{w}^\mu}{\partial x_\mu} \equiv \mathfrak{W}_\mu^\mu$$

$$\frac{\partial\mathfrak{W}_\nu^\mu}{\partial x_\mu} - \Gamma_{\nu\beta}^\alpha\mathfrak{W}_\alpha^\beta \equiv$$

$$\xi + \frac{\beta(r'_0 - r')}{lc} = \beta^2\frac{v\xi}{c^2} + \frac{\beta}{lc}\left(\xi\frac{\partial r'}{\partial x} + \eta\frac{\partial r'}{\partial y} + \zeta\frac{\partial r'}{\partial z}\right)$$

$$A_\mu = \frac{\partial\phi}{\partial x_\mu}$$

$$\frac{\partial^2\gamma_{\mu\nu}}{\partial x_\alpha{}^2} = 2\kappa T_{\mu\nu}^*$$

$$P_x = \int\rho\xi dS, \quad P_y = \int\rho\eta dS, \quad P_z = \int\rho\zeta dS$$

$$\begin{bmatrix}\mu\nu\\\alpha\end{bmatrix} = g_{\alpha\beta}\Gamma_{\mu\nu}^\beta$$

$$\frac{dP_x}{dt} = \int\rho u_x dS, \quad \frac{dP_y}{dt} = \int\rho u_y dS, \quad \frac{dP_z}{dt} = \int$$

$$u_\xi = \frac{u_x - v}{1 - u_x v/c^2}$$

$$u_\eta = \frac{u_y}{\beta(1 - u_x v/c^2)}$$

$$\int K_1 dx_1 dx_2 dx_3 = \int\frac{\partial T_{14}}{\partial x_4}dx_1 d$$

$$u_\zeta = \frac{u_z}{\beta(1 - u_x v/c^2)},$$

$$\begin{bmatrix}\mu\nu\\\alpha\end{bmatrix} = g_{\alpha\beta}\Gamma_{\mu\nu}^\beta$$

$$\rho' = \frac{\partial X'}{\partial\xi} + \frac{\partial Y'}{\partial\eta} + \frac{\partial Z'}{\partial\zeta}$$
$$= \beta(1 - u_x v/c^2)\rho.$$

Bite-Size
Einstein

Quotations on Just About Everything from the
Greatest Mind of the Twentieth Century

COMPILED BY JERRY MAYER AND JOHN P. HOLMS

St. Martin's Press ❧ New York

A Thomas Dunne Book.

An Imprint of St. Martin's Press.

Design by Bonni Leon-Berman

Library of Congress Cataloging-in-Publication Data

Einstein, Albert, 1879–1955.
  Bite-size Einstein: quotations on just about everything from the
  greatest mind of the twentieth century / compiled by Jerry Mayer
  and John P. Holms. —1st ed.
      p.   cm.
    ISBN 0-312-14551-9
    1. Einstein, Albert, 1879–1955—Quotations. I. Mayer, Jerry,
1941– . II. Holms, John P. III. Title.
QC16.E5A25 1996b
081— dc20   96-18830
                                                                 CIP

10 9 8 7 6 5 4 3 2

There's a wonderful family named Stein,

There's Ep, there's Gert, and there's Ein.

Ep's statues are junk, Gert's poems are bunk,

And nobody understands Ein.

—*Anonymous*

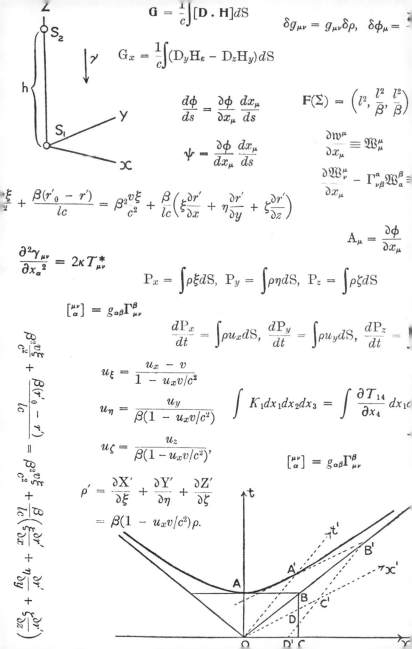

$$\mathbf{G} = \frac{1}{c}\int [\mathbf{D} \cdot \mathbf{H}]dS$$

$$\delta g_{\mu\nu} = g_{\mu\nu}\delta\rho, \quad \delta\phi_\mu =$$

$$G_x = \frac{1}{c}\int (D_y H_z - D_z H_y)dS$$

$$\frac{d\phi}{ds} = \frac{\partial\phi}{\partial x_\mu}\frac{dx_\mu}{ds}$$

$$\mathbf{F}(\Sigma) = \left(l^2, \frac{l^2}{\beta}, \frac{l^2}{\beta}\right)$$

$$\psi = \frac{\partial\phi}{\partial x_\mu}\frac{dx_\mu}{ds}$$

$$\frac{\partial \mathfrak{w}^\mu}{\partial x_\mu} \equiv \mathfrak{W}^\mu_\mu$$

$$\frac{\partial \mathfrak{W}^\mu_\nu}{\partial x_\mu} - \Gamma^\alpha_{\nu\beta}\mathfrak{W}^\beta_\alpha \equiv$$

$$\frac{\xi}{z} + \frac{\beta(r'_0 - r')}{lc} = \beta^2\frac{v\xi}{c^2} + \frac{\beta}{lc}\left(\xi\frac{\partial r'}{\partial x} + \eta\frac{\partial r'}{\partial y} + \zeta\frac{\partial r'}{\partial z}\right)$$

$$\frac{\partial^2\gamma_{\mu\nu}}{\partial x_\alpha^2} = 2\kappa T^*_{\mu\nu}$$

$$A_\mu = \frac{\partial\phi}{\partial x_\mu}$$

$$P_x = \int\rho\xi dS, \quad P_y = \int\rho\eta dS, \quad P_z = \int\rho\zeta dS$$

$$\begin{bmatrix}\mu\nu\\\alpha\end{bmatrix} = g_{\alpha\beta}\Gamma^\beta_{\mu\nu}$$

$$\frac{dP_x}{dt} = \int\rho u_x dS, \quad \frac{dP_y}{dt} = \int\rho u_y dS, \quad \frac{dP_z}{dt} =$$

$$\frac{\beta^2}{c^2}\frac{v\xi}{ } + \frac{\beta(r'_0 - r')}{lc} = \beta^2\frac{v\xi}{c^2} + \frac{\beta}{lc}\left(\xi\frac{\partial r'}{\partial x} + \eta\frac{\partial r'}{\partial y} + \zeta\frac{\partial r'}{\partial z}\right)$$

$$u_\xi = \frac{u_x - v}{1 - u_x v/c^2}$$

$$u_\eta = \frac{u_y}{\beta(1 - u_x v/c^2)}$$

$$\int K_1 dx_1 dx_2 dx_3 = \int \frac{\partial T_{14}}{\partial x_4} dx_1 d$$

$$u_\zeta = \frac{u_z}{\beta(1 - u_x v/c^2)},$$

$$\begin{bmatrix}\mu\nu\\\alpha\end{bmatrix} = g_{\alpha\beta}\Gamma^\beta_{\mu\nu}$$

$$\rho' = \frac{\partial X'}{\partial \xi} + \frac{\partial Y'}{\partial \eta} + \frac{\partial Z'}{\partial \zeta}$$

$$= \beta(1 - u_x v/c^2)\rho.$$

Thanks to Tony and Jeremy for being part of the equation and thanks to Al, who made it all relative and is, in fact, a funny guy.

—JPH & JM

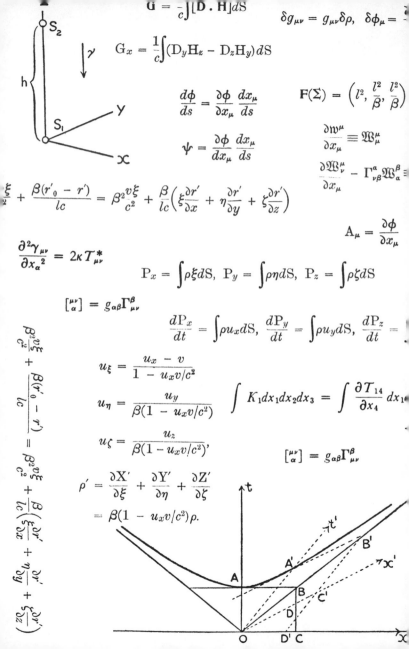

$$\mathbf{G} = \frac{1}{c}\int [\mathbf{D} \cdot \mathbf{H}]dS$$

$$\delta g_{\mu\nu} = g_{\mu\nu}\delta\rho, \quad \delta\phi_\mu = \text{?}$$

$$G_x = \frac{1}{c}\int (D_y H_z - D_z H_y)\,dS$$

$$\frac{d\phi}{ds} = \frac{\partial\phi}{\partial x_\mu}\frac{dx_\mu}{ds}$$

$$\mathbf{F}(\Sigma) = \left(l^2, \frac{l^2}{\beta}, \frac{l^2}{\beta}\right)$$

$$\psi = \frac{\partial\phi}{\partial x_\mu}\frac{dx_\mu}{ds}$$

$$\frac{\partial \mathfrak{w}^\mu}{\partial x_\mu} \equiv \mathfrak{W}^\mu_\mu$$

$$\frac{\partial \mathfrak{W}^\mu_\nu}{\partial x_\mu} - \Gamma^a_{\nu\beta}\mathfrak{W}^\beta_a \equiv$$

$$\frac{\xi}{2} + \frac{\beta(r'_0 - r')}{lc} = \beta^2\frac{v\xi}{c^2} + \frac{\beta}{lc}\left(\xi\frac{\partial r'}{\partial x} + \eta\frac{\partial r'}{\partial y} + \zeta\frac{\partial r'}{\partial z}\right)$$

$$A_\mu = \frac{\partial\phi}{\partial x_\mu}$$

$$\frac{\partial^2\gamma_{\mu\nu}}{\partial x_\alpha^2} = 2\kappa T^*_{\mu\nu}$$

$$P_x = \int \rho\xi dS, \quad P_y = \int \rho\eta dS, \quad P_z = \int \rho\zeta dS$$

$$\begin{bmatrix}\mu\nu\\\alpha\end{bmatrix} = g_{\alpha\beta}\Gamma^\beta_{\mu\nu}$$

$$\frac{dP_x}{dt} = \int \rho u_x dS, \quad \frac{dP_y}{dt} = \int \rho u_y dS, \quad \frac{dP_z}{dt} =$$

$$\frac{\beta^2}{c^2}\frac{v\xi}{} + \frac{\beta(r'_0 - r')}{lc} = \beta^2\frac{v\xi}{c^2} + \frac{\beta}{lc}\left(\xi\frac{\partial r'}{\partial x} + \eta\frac{\partial r'}{\partial y} + \zeta\frac{\partial r'}{\partial z}\right)$$

$$u_\xi = \frac{u_x - v}{1 - u_x v/c^2}$$

$$u_\eta = \frac{u_y}{\beta(1 - u_x v/c^2)}$$

$$\int K_1 dx_1 dx_2 dx_3 = \int \frac{\partial T_{14}}{\partial x_4}\,dx_1$$

$$u_\zeta = \frac{u_z}{\beta(1 - u_x v/c^2)},$$

$$\begin{bmatrix}\mu\nu\\\alpha\end{bmatrix} = g_{\alpha\beta}\Gamma^\beta_{\mu\nu}$$

$$\rho' = \frac{\partial X'}{\partial\xi} + \frac{\partial Y'}{\partial\eta} + \frac{\partial Z'}{\partial\zeta}$$
$$= \beta(1 - u_x v/c^2)\rho.$$

ABOUT TEN YEARS AGO I spoke with Einstein about the astounding fact that so many ministers of various denominations are strongly interested in the theory of relativity. Einstein said that according to his estimation there are more clergymen interested in relativity than physicists. A little puzzled I asked him how he could explain this strange fact. He answered, smiling a little, "Because clergymen are interested in the general laws of nature and physicists, very often are not."

—*Philippe Frank, theoretical physicist, 1949*

CONTENTS

$$G = \frac{1}{c}\int[\mathbf{D}\cdot\mathbf{H}]dS$$

$$\delta g_{\mu\nu} = g_{\mu\nu}\delta\rho, \quad \delta\phi_\mu = \frac{\partial(}{\partial}$$

$$G_x = \frac{1}{c}\int(D_y H_z - D_z H_y)\,dS$$

$$\frac{d\phi}{ds} = \frac{\partial\phi}{\partial x_\mu}\frac{dx_\mu}{ds}$$

$$\mathbf{F}(\Sigma) = \left(l^2, \frac{l^2}{\beta}, \frac{l^2}{\beta}\right)\mathbf{F}$$

$$\psi = \frac{\partial\phi}{\partial x_\mu}\frac{dx_\mu}{ds}$$

$$\frac{\partial\mathfrak{w}^\mu}{\partial x_\mu} \equiv \mathfrak{W}^\mu_\mu$$

$$\frac{\partial\mathfrak{W}^\mu_\nu}{\partial x_\mu} - \Gamma^\alpha_{\nu\beta}\mathfrak{W}^\beta_\alpha \equiv$$

$$+ \frac{\beta(r'_0 - r')}{lc} = \beta^2\frac{v\xi}{c^2} + \frac{\beta}{lc}\left(\xi\frac{\partial r'}{\partial x} + \eta\frac{\partial r'}{\partial y} + \zeta\frac{\partial r'}{\partial z}\right)$$

$$\frac{\partial^2\gamma_{\mu\nu}}{\partial x_\alpha^2} = 2\kappa T^*_{\mu\nu}$$

$$A_\mu = \frac{\partial\phi}{\partial x_\mu}$$

$$P_x = \int\rho\xi dS, \quad P_y = \int\rho\eta dS, \quad P_z = \int\rho\zeta dS$$

$$\begin{bmatrix}\mu\nu\\\alpha\end{bmatrix} = g_{\alpha\beta}\Gamma^\beta_{\mu\nu}$$

$$\frac{dP_x}{dt} = \int\rho u_x dS, \quad \frac{dP_y}{dt} = \int\rho u_y dS, \quad \frac{dP_z}{dt} = \int\rho$$

$$u_\xi = \frac{u_x - v}{1 - u_x v/c^2}$$

$$u_\eta = \frac{u_y}{\beta(1 - u_x v/c^2)}$$

$$\int K_1 dx_1 dx_2 dx_3 = \int\frac{\partial T_{14}}{\partial x_4}dx_1 dx_2$$

$$u_\zeta = \frac{u_z}{\beta(1 - u_x v/c^2)},$$

$$-\imath$$

$$\begin{bmatrix}\mu\nu\\\alpha\end{bmatrix} = g_{\alpha\beta}\Gamma^\beta_{\mu\nu}$$

$$\rho' = \frac{\partial X'}{\partial\xi} + \frac{\partial Y'}{\partial\eta} + \frac{\partial Z'}{\partial\zeta}$$

$$= \beta(1 - u_x v/c^2)\rho.$$

$$\beta^2\frac{v\xi}{c^2} + \frac{\beta(r'_0 - r')}{lc} = \beta^2\frac{v\xi}{c^2} + \frac{\beta}{lc}\left(\xi\frac{\partial r'}{\partial x} + \eta\frac{\partial r'}{\partial y} + \zeta\frac{\partial r'}{\partial z}\right)$$

WHEREVER I GO AND wherever I stay,

There's always a picture of me on display.

On top of the desk, or out in the hall,

Tied round a neck, or hung on the wall.

WOMEN AND MEN, they play a strange game,

Asking, beseeching: "Please sign your name."

From the erudite fellow they brook not a quibble,

But firmly insist on a piece of his scribble.

SOMETIMES, surrounded by all this good cheer,

I'm puzzled by some of the things that I hear,

And wonder, my mind for a moment not hazy,

If I and not they could really be crazy.

—Albert Einstein

Bite-Size

Einstein

ON ART AND MUSIC

$$G = -\frac{1}{c}\int [D \cdot H] dS$$

$$\delta g_{\mu\nu} = g_{\mu\nu}\delta\rho, \quad \delta\phi_\mu = \frac{\partial(}{\partial}$$

$$G_x = \frac{1}{c}\int (D_y H_z - D_z H_y) dS$$

$$\frac{d\phi}{ds} = \frac{\partial\phi}{\partial x_\mu}\frac{dx_\mu}{ds} \qquad \mathbf{F}(\Sigma) = \left(l^2, \frac{l^2}{\beta}, \frac{l^2}{\beta}\right)\mathbf{F}$$

$$\psi = \frac{\partial\phi}{\partial x_\mu}\frac{dx_\mu}{ds} \qquad \frac{\partial \mathfrak{w}^\mu}{\partial x_\mu} \equiv \mathfrak{W}_\mu^\mu$$

$$\frac{\partial \mathfrak{W}_\nu^\mu}{\partial x_\mu} - \Gamma_{\nu\beta}^\alpha \mathfrak{W}_\alpha^\beta \equiv$$

$$+ \frac{\beta(r'_0 - r')}{lc} = \beta^2\frac{v\xi}{c^2} + \frac{\beta}{lc}\left(\xi\frac{\partial r'}{\partial x} + \eta\frac{\partial r'}{\partial y} + \zeta\frac{\partial r'}{\partial z}\right)$$

$$A_\mu = \frac{\partial\phi}{\partial x_\mu}$$

$$\frac{\partial^2\gamma_{\mu\nu}}{\partial x_\alpha^2} = 2\kappa T_{\mu\nu}^*$$

$$P_x = \int\rho\xi dS, \quad P_y = \int\rho\eta dS, \quad P_z = \int\rho\zeta dS$$

$$\left[\begin{matrix}\mu\nu\\\alpha\end{matrix}\right] = g_{\alpha\beta}\Gamma_{\mu\nu}^\beta$$

$$\frac{dP_x}{dt} = \int\rho u_x dS, \quad \frac{dP_y}{dt} = \int\rho u_y dS, \quad \frac{dP_z}{dt} = \int\rho$$

$$u_\xi = \frac{u_x - v}{1 - u_x v/c^2}$$

$$u_\eta = \frac{u_y}{\beta(1 - u_x v/c^2)} \qquad \int K_1 dx_1 dx_2 dx_3 = \int \frac{\partial T_{14}}{\partial x_4} dx_1 dx$$

$$u_\zeta = \frac{u_z}{\beta(1 - u_x v/c^2)},$$

$$\left[\begin{matrix}\mu\nu\\\alpha\end{matrix}\right] = g_{\alpha\beta}\Gamma_{\mu\nu}^\beta$$

$$\rho' = \frac{\partial X'}{\partial\xi} + \frac{\partial Y'}{\partial\eta} + \frac{\partial Z'}{\partial\zeta}$$

$$= \beta(1 - u_x v/c^2)\rho.$$

What applies to jokes I suppose also applies to pictures and to plays. I think they should not smell of logical scheme, but of a delicious fragment of life, scintillating with various colors, according to the position of the beholder. If one wants to get away from this vagueness, one must take up mathematics.

In music I do not look for logic. I am quite intuitive on the whole and know no theories.

[On Richard Strauss]: Gifted, but without inner truth.

This is what I have to say about Bach's life work: listen, play, love, revere — and keep your mouth shut.

Handel is good—even perfect—but he has a certain shallowness.

True art is characterized by an irresistible urge in the creative artist. I can feel this urge in Ernst Bloch's work as in few later musicians.

[On Beethoven]: For me too dramatic and too personal.

[On Brahms]: Most of his works have for me no inner persuasiveness. I do not understand why it was necessary to write them.

I admire Wagner's inventiveness, but I see his lack of architectural structure as decadence. Moreover, to me his musical personality is indescribably offensive, so that for the most part I can listen to him only with disgust.

[On Schumann]: Attractive in his smaller works.

[On Felix Mendelssohn]: Considerable talent but an indefinable lack of depth that often leads to banality.

Culture in its higher forms is a delicate plant.

Mastery demands all of a person. Toscanini demonstrates this in every manifestation of his life.

[On George Bernard Shaw]: Only to a tiny minority is it given to fascinate their generation by subtle humor and grace and to hold the mirror up to it by the impersonal agency of art. Today I salute with sincere emotion the supreme master of the method, who has delighted—and educated—us all.

One flower is beautiful, a surfeit of flowers is vulgar.

Music does not influence research work, but both are nourished by the same source of longing, and they complement one another in the release they offer.

If I were not a physicist, I would probably be a musician. I often think in music. I live my daydreams in music. I see my life in terms of music . . . I get most joy in life out of music.

I am enough of an artist to draw freely upon my imagination.

Einstein

ON ETHICS AND MORALITY

$$G = \frac{1}{c}\int [D \cdot H]\,dS$$

$$\delta g_{\mu\nu} = g_{\mu\nu}\delta\rho, \quad \delta\phi_\mu = \frac{\partial(\delta\rho}{\partial x_k}$$

$$G_x = \frac{1}{c}\int (D_y H_z - D_z H_y)\,dS$$

$$\frac{d\phi}{ds} = \frac{\partial\phi}{\partial x_\mu}\frac{dx_\mu}{ds}$$

$$F(\Sigma) = \left(l^2, \frac{l^2}{\beta}, \frac{l^2}{\beta}\right)F(\Sigma$$

$$\psi = \frac{\partial\phi}{\partial x_\mu}\frac{dx_\mu}{ds}$$

$$\frac{\partial w^\alpha}{\partial x_\mu} \equiv \mathfrak{W}_\mu^\mu$$

$$\frac{\partial\mathfrak{W}_\nu^\mu}{\partial x_\mu} - \Gamma_{\nu\beta}^\alpha \mathfrak{W}_\alpha^\beta \equiv \tfrac{1}{2}$$

$$\frac{\beta(r'_0 - r')}{lc} = \beta^2\frac{v\xi}{c^2} + \frac{\beta}{lc}\left(\xi\frac{\partial r'}{\partial x} + \eta\frac{\partial r'}{\partial y} + \zeta\frac{\partial r'}{\partial z}\right)$$

$$\frac{\partial^2\gamma_{\mu\nu}}{\partial x_\alpha^2} = 2\kappa T_{\mu\nu}^*$$

$$P_x = \int\rho\xi\,dS, \quad P_y = \int\rho\eta\,dS, \quad P_z = \int\rho\zeta\,dS$$

$$[^{\mu\nu}_\alpha] = g_{\alpha\beta}\Gamma_{\mu\nu}^\beta$$

$$\frac{dP_x}{dt} = \int\rho u_x\,dS, \quad \frac{dP_y}{dt} = \int\rho u_y\,dS, \quad \frac{dP_z}{dt} = \int\rho u$$

$$u_\xi = \frac{u_x - v}{1 - u_x v/c^2}$$

$$u_\eta = \frac{u_y}{\beta(1 - u_x v/c^2)}$$

$$\int K_1 dx_1 dx_2 dx_3 = \int \frac{\partial T_{14}}{\partial x_4}\,dx_1 dx_2$$

$$u_\zeta = \frac{u_z}{\beta(1 - u_x v/c^2)},$$

$$-i$$

$$[^{\mu\nu}_\alpha] = g_{\alpha\beta}\Gamma_{\mu\nu}^\beta$$

$$\rho' = \frac{\partial X'}{\partial\xi} + \frac{\partial Y'}{\partial\eta} + \frac{\partial Z'}{\partial\zeta}$$

$$= \beta(1 - u_x v/c^2)\rho.$$

People of our type see in morality a purely human matter, albeit the most important in the human sphere.

Ethics is a science about moral values, but not a science to discover moral "truths."

I do not believe in immortality of the individual, and I consider ethics to be an exclusively human concern with no superhuman authority behind it.

The foundation of all human values is morality. To have recognized this is the unique greatness of our Moses. In contrast, look at the people today!

Morality is of the highest importance—but for us, not for God.

Do not pride yourself on the few great men who, over the centuries, have been born on your earth—through no merit of yours. Reflect, rather, on how you treated them at the time, and how you have followed their teachings.

Nothing truly valuable arises from ambition or from a mere sense of duty; it stems rather from love and devotion towards men and towards objective things.

The foundation of morality should not be made dependent on myth nor tied to any authority lest doubt about the myth or about the legitimacy of the authority imperil the foundation of sound judgment and action.

Nothing will benefit human health and increase the chances for survival of life on Earth as much as the evolution to a vegetarian diet.

A human being is part of the whole called by us universe, a part limited in time and space. We experience ourselves, our thoughts, and feelings as something separate from the rest. A kind of optical delusion of consciousness. This delusion is a kind of prison for us, restricting us to our personal desires and to affection for a few persons nearest to us. Our task must be to free ourselves from the prison by widening our circle of compassion to embrace all living creatures and the whole of nature in its beauty... We shall require a substantially new manner of thinking if mankind is to survive.

The most important human endeavor is the striving for morality in our actions. Our inner balance and even our very existence depend on it. Only morality in our actions can give beauty and dignity to life.

Comfort and happiness have never appeared to me as a goal. I call these ethical bases the ideal of the swineherd.

In the service of life sacrifice becomes grace.

Nowhere have we really overcome what Thorstein Veblen called "the predatory phase" of human development.

Einstein

The destiny of civilized humanity depends more than ever on the moral forces it is capable of generating.

Where the pure see purity, the pig sees smut.

The commonplace goals of human endeavor—possessions, outward success and luxury have always seemed to me despicable, since early youth.

I prefer silent vice to ostentatious virtue.

We do things, but we do not know why we do them.

Humanity is more important than national citizenship.

ON HIMSELF

$$G = \frac{1}{c}\int [\mathbf{D} . \mathbf{H}]dS$$

$$\delta g_{\mu\nu} = g_{\mu\nu}\delta\rho, \quad \delta\phi_\mu = \frac{\dots}{\dots}$$

$$G_x = \frac{1}{c}\int (D_y H_z - D_z H_y)\,dS$$

$$\frac{d\phi}{ds} = \frac{\partial\phi}{\partial x_\mu}\frac{dx_\mu}{ds}$$

$$F(\Sigma) = \left(l^2, \frac{l^2}{\beta}, \frac{l^2}{\beta}\right)$$

$$\psi = \frac{\partial\phi}{\partial x_\mu}\frac{dx_\mu}{ds}$$

$$\frac{\partial w^\mu}{\partial x_\mu} \equiv \mathfrak{W}^\mu_\mu$$

$$\frac{\partial \mathfrak{W}^\mu_\nu}{\partial x_\mu} - \Gamma^\alpha_{\nu\beta}\mathfrak{W}^\beta_\alpha =$$

$$\xi + \frac{\beta(r'_0 - r')}{lc} = \beta^2\frac{v\xi}{c^2} + \frac{\beta}{lc}\left(\xi\frac{\partial r'}{\partial x} + \eta\frac{\partial r'}{\partial y} + \zeta\frac{\partial r'}{\partial z}\right)$$

$$A_\mu = \frac{\partial\phi}{\partial x_\mu}$$

$$\frac{\partial^2\gamma_{\mu\nu}}{\partial x_\alpha^2} = 2\kappa T^*_{\mu\nu}$$

$$P_x = \int\rho\xi dS, \quad P_y = \int\rho\eta dS, \quad P_z = \int\rho\zeta dS$$

$$\left[\begin{smallmatrix}\mu\nu\\\alpha\end{smallmatrix}\right] = g_{\alpha\beta}\Gamma^\beta_{\mu\nu}$$

$$\frac{dP_x}{dt} = \int\rho u_x dS, \quad \frac{dP_y}{dt} = \int\rho u_y dS, \quad \frac{dP_z}{dt} =$$

$$u_\xi = \frac{u_x - v}{1 - u_x v/c^2}$$

$$u_\eta = \frac{u_y}{\beta(1 - u_x v/c^2)}$$

$$\int K_1 dx_1 dx_2 dx_3 = \int \frac{\partial T_{14}}{\partial x_4} dx_1$$

$$u_\zeta = \frac{u_z}{\beta(1 - u_x v/c^2)},$$

$$\left[\begin{smallmatrix}\mu\nu\\\alpha\end{smallmatrix}\right] = g_{\alpha\beta}\Gamma^\beta_{\mu\nu}$$

$$\rho' = \frac{\partial X'}{\partial\xi} + \frac{\partial Y'}{\partial\eta} + \frac{\partial Z'}{\partial\zeta}$$

$$= \beta(1 - u_x v/c^2)\rho.$$

[To his niece]: I hear from Elsa that you are dissatisfied because you did not see your Uncle Einstein. Let me therefore tell you what I look like: pale face, long hair, and a tiny beginning of a paunch. In addition an awkward gait, and a cigar in the mouth—if he happens to have a cigar—and a pen in his pocket or his hand. But crooked legs and warts he does not have, and so he is quite handsome—also no hair on his hands as is often found on ugly men. So it is indeed a pity that you did not see me. With warm greetings from Your Uncle Einstein.

I collect nothing but unanswered correspondence and people, who, with justification, are dissatisfied with me. But can it be otherwise with a man possessed. As in my youth, I sit here endlessly and think and calculate, hoping to unearth deep secrets. The so-called Great World, that is, men's bustle, has less attraction than ever, so that each day I find myself becoming more of a hermit.

I am truly a "lone traveler."

With fame I became more and more stupid, which, of course, is a very common phenomenon. There is far too great a disproportion between what one is and what others think one is, or at least what they say they think one is. But one has to take it all with good humor.

All I have is the stubbornness of a mule; no, that's not quite all, I also have a nose.

With me, every peep becomes a trumpet solo.

Yesterday idolized, today hated and spit upon, tomorrow forgotten, and the day after tomorrow promoted to Sainthood. The only salvation is a sense of humor, and we will keep that as long as we draw breath.

I live in that solitude that is painful in youth but delicious in the years of maturity.

It was no different in Berlin, and before that in Switzerland. One is born a loner.

To one bent by age death will come as a release; I feel this quite strongly now that I have grown old myself and have come to regard death like an old debt, at long last to be discharged.

It's not that I'm so smart; it's just that I stay with problems longer.

I have no special gift. I am only passionately curious.

Everything that has anything to do with the cult of personality has always been painful to me.

Neckties and cuffs exist for me only as remote memories.

Einstein

In the course of my long life I have received from my fellow men far more recognition than I deserve, and I confess that my sense of shame has always outweighed my pleasure therein.

People flatter me as long as I do not get in their way.

Here is yet another application of the principle of relativity for the delectation of the reader: today I am described in Germany as a "German savant," and in England as a "Swiss Jew." Should it ever be my fate to be represented as a bête noire, I should, on the contrary, become a "Swiss Jew" for the Germans and a "German savant" for the English.

My part in producing the atomic bomb consisted in a single act: I signed a letter to President Roosevelt, to press the need for experiments on a large scale in order to explore the possibilities for the production of an atomic bomb. The likelihood that the Germans were working on the same problem with a chance of succeeding forced me to this step.

I have never belonged wholeheartedly to any country or state, to my circle of friends, or even to my own family. These ties have always been accompanied by a vague aloofness, and the wish to withdraw into myself increases with the years.

I've had good ideas, and so have other men. But it's been my good fortune that my ideas have been accepted.

I am the Jewish Saint.

I made one great mistake in my life when I signed the letter to President Roosevelt recommending that atom bombs be made; but there was some justification—the danger that the Germans would make them.

The only way to escape the personal corruption of praise is to go on working. One is tempted to stop and listen to it. The only thing is to turn away and go on working. Work. There is nothing else.

Einstein

[At a dinner in his honor]: I thank you for all the things you have said of me. If I believed them I would not be sane, and since I know I am sane, I do not believe them.

I am happy because I want nothing from anyone. I do not care for money. Decorations, titles, or distinctions mean nothing to me. I do not crave praise. The only thing that gives me pleasure, apart from my work, my violin, and my sailboat, is the appreciation of my fellow-workers.

My power, my particular ability, lies in visualizing the effects, consequences and possibilities, and the bearings on present thought of the discoveries of others. I grasp things in a broad way easily. I cannot do mathematical calculations easily. I do them not willingly and not readily. Others perform these details better.

ON LIFE

$$G = \frac{1}{c}\int [\mathbf{D} \cdot \mathbf{H}] dS$$

$$\delta g_{\mu\nu} = g_{\mu\nu}\delta\rho, \quad \delta\phi_\mu =$$

$$G_x = \frac{1}{c}\int (D_y H_z - D_z H_y) dS$$

$$\frac{d\phi}{ds} = \frac{\partial\phi}{\partial x_\mu}\frac{dx_\mu}{ds}$$

$$F(\Sigma) = \left(l^2, \frac{l^2}{\beta}, \frac{l^2}{\beta}\right)$$

$$\psi = \frac{\partial\phi}{\partial x_\mu}\frac{dx_\mu}{ds}$$

$$\frac{\partial \mathfrak{w}^\mu}{\partial x_\mu} \equiv \mathfrak{W}^\mu_\mu$$

$$\frac{\partial \mathfrak{W}^\mu_\nu}{\partial x_\mu} - \Gamma^\alpha_{\nu\beta}\mathfrak{W}^\beta_\alpha =$$

$$\xi + \frac{\beta(r'_0 - r')}{lc} = \beta^2\frac{v\xi}{c^2} + \frac{\beta}{lc}\left(\xi\frac{\partial r'}{\partial x} + \eta\frac{\partial r'}{\partial y} + \zeta\frac{\partial r'}{\partial z}\right)$$

$$A_\mu = \frac{\partial\phi}{\partial x_\mu}$$

$$\frac{\partial^2\gamma_{\mu\nu}}{\partial x_\alpha{}^2} = 2\kappa T^*_{\mu\nu}$$

$$P_x = \int\rho\xi dS, \quad P_y = \int\rho\eta dS, \quad P_z = \int\rho\zeta dS$$

$$\left[\begin{smallmatrix}\mu\nu\\\alpha\end{smallmatrix}\right] = g_{\alpha\beta}\Gamma^\beta_{\mu\nu}$$

$$\frac{dP_x}{dt} = \int\rho u_x dS, \quad \frac{dP_y}{dt} = \int\rho u_y dS, \quad \frac{dP_z}{dt} =$$

$$u_\xi = \frac{u_x - v}{1 - u_x v/c^2}$$

$$u_\eta = \frac{u_y}{\beta(1 - u_x v/c^2)}$$

$$\int K_1 dx_1 dx_2 dx_3 = \int \frac{\partial T_{14}}{\partial x_4} dx_1 c$$

$$u_\zeta = \frac{u_z}{\beta(1 - u_x v/c^2)},$$

$$\left[\begin{smallmatrix}\mu\nu\\\alpha\end{smallmatrix}\right] = g_{\alpha\beta}\Gamma^\beta_{\mu\nu}$$

$$\rho' = \frac{\partial X'}{\partial\xi} + \frac{\partial Y'}{\partial\eta} + \frac{\partial Z'}{\partial\zeta}$$
$$= \beta(1 - u_x v/c^2)\rho.$$

What a peculiar way this is to weather the storms of life—in many a lucid moment I appear to myself as an ostrich who buries his head in the desert sand so as not to perceive the danger. One creates a small little world for oneself, and as lamentably insignificant as it may be in comparison with the ever-changing greatness of real existence, one feels miraculously large and important, just like a mole in his self-dug hole.

My scientific work is motivated by an irresistible longing to understand the secrets of nature and by no other feelings. My love for justice and the striving to contribute toward the improvement of human conditions are quite independent from my scientific interests.

The sea has a look of indescribable grandeur, especially when the sun falls on it. One feels as if one is dissolved and merged into Nature. Even more than usual, one feels the insignificance of the individual, and it makes one happy.

Why denigrate oneself? Others take care of that when necessary.

I regret that I cannot accede to your request, because I should like very much to remain in the darkness of not having been analyzed. [On a request from an analyst that Einstein allow himself to be psychoanalyzed.]

One is born into a herd of buffaloes and must be glad if one is not trampled underfoot before one's time.

The true value of a human being is determined primarily by the measure and the sense in which he has attained liberation from the self.

Two things inspire me to awe—the starry heavens above and the moral universe within.

We should take care not to make the intellect our god; it has, of course, powerful muscles, but no personality.

Without deep reflection one knows from daily life that one exists for other people.

A hundred times every day I remind myself that my inner and outer life are based on the labors of others.

Only a life lived for others is a life worthwhile.

Sometimes one pays most for the things one gets for nothing. If I had my life to live over again, I'd be a plumber.

Common sense is the collection of prejudices acquired by age eighteen.

Einstein

Falling in love is not at all the most stupid thing that people do—but gravitation cannot be held responsible for it.

I never think of the future—it comes soon enough.

It is really a puzzle what drives one to take one's work so devilishly seriously. For whom? For oneself?—one soon leaves, after all. For one's contemporaries? For posterity? *No*, it remains a puzzle.

Never lose a holy curiosity.

Make friends with a few animals. Then you will become a cheerful man once more and nothing will be able to trouble you.

Bureaucracy is the death of any achievement.

There is much truth in the saying that it is easy to give just and wise counsel—to others!—but hard to act justly and wisely for oneself.

I was supposed to choose a practical profession, but this was simply unbearable to me.

Work is the only thing that gives substance to life.
After all, our goals are merely soap bubbles.
We are all two-legged animals descended from the apes.

I can die without the help of doctors.

The people of northern Italy are the most civilized people I have ever met.

Einstein

In my relativity theory I set up a clock at every point in space, but in reality I find it difficult to provide even one clock in my room.

My wife does my mathematics.

The filthier a nation is, the tougher it is.

I'm glad my wife doesn't know any science; my first wife did.

Only when we are born and when we die are we permitted to act in an honest way.

It is interesting how even the closest of family ties dwindle into habitual friendship. Deep inside we no longer understand one another, and are incapable of actively empathizing with the other, or knowing what emotions move the other.

I have come to know the mutability of all human relations and learned to isolate myself from heat and cold so that the temperature balance is fairly well assured.

I know a little about nature and hardly anything about men.

God never tells us in advance whether the course we are to follow is the correct one.

The end comes sometime: Does it matter when?

Einstein

Curiosity has its own reason for existence. One cannot help but be in awe when one contemplates the mysteries of eternity, of life, of the marvelous structure of reality. It is enough if one tries merely to comprehend a little of this mystery each day.

My mother is of a good disposition, on the whole, but a true devil as mother-in-law. When she is with us then everything is filled with dynamite.

People are like the ocean: sometimes smooth and friendly, at others stormy and full of malice. The important thing to remember is that they too are mostly made of water.

Misfortune suits humanity incomparably better than success.

Everyone has to sacrifice at the altar of stupidity from time to time, to please the Deity and the human race.

Physicists are all a bit crazy, aren't they? But it's just the same with racehorses: what one buys one has to sell.

Egoism and competition are, alas, stronger forces than public spirit and sense of duty.

I do not mind that you are a girl, but the main thing is that you yourself do not mind. There is no reason for it.

Biological procedures cannot be expressed in mathematical formulae.

Being occupied with the opposite sex is as delightful as it is necessary, but it must not become one of the main tenors of life, otherwise the person is lost.

E i n s t e i n

What a strange thing must be a girl's soul! Do you really believe that you could find permanent happiness through others, even if this be the one and only beloved man? I know this sort of animal personally, from my own experience, as I am one of them myself. Not too much should be expected from them, this I know quite exactly.

Marriage is the unsuccessful attempt to make something lasting out of an incident.

When women are in their homes, they are attached to their furniture. They run round it all day long and are always fussing over it. But when I am with a woman on a journey, I am the only piece of furniture she has available, and she cannot refrain from moving round me all day long and improving something about me.

ON PHILOSOPHY

$$G = \frac{1}{c}\int [\mathbf{D} \cdot \mathbf{H}]dS$$

$$\delta g_{\mu\nu} = g_{\mu\nu}\delta\rho, \quad \delta\phi_\mu = \delta$$

$$G_x = \frac{1}{c}\int (D_y H_z - D_z H_y)dS$$

$$\frac{d\phi}{ds} = \frac{\partial\phi}{\partial x_\mu}\frac{dx_\mu}{ds}$$

$$\mathbf{F}(\Sigma) = \left(l^2, \frac{l^2}{\beta}, \frac{l^2}{\beta}\right)$$

$$\psi = \frac{\partial\phi}{\partial x_\mu}\frac{dx_\mu}{ds}$$

$$\frac{\partial w^\mu}{\partial x_\mu} \equiv \mathfrak{W}^\mu_\mu$$

$$\frac{\partial\mathfrak{W}^\mu_\nu}{\partial x_\mu} - \Gamma^\alpha_{\nu\beta}\mathfrak{W}^\beta_\alpha \equiv$$

$$+ \frac{\beta(r'_0 - r')}{lc} = \beta^2\frac{v\xi}{c^2} + \frac{\beta}{lc}\left(\xi\frac{\partial r'}{\partial x} + \eta\frac{\partial r'}{\partial y} + \zeta\frac{\partial r'}{\partial z}\right)$$

$$A_\mu = \frac{\partial\phi}{\partial x_\mu}$$

$$\frac{\partial^2\gamma_{\mu\nu}}{\partial x_\alpha^2} = 2\kappa T^*_{\mu\nu}$$

$$P_x = \int\rho\xi dS, \quad P_y = \int\rho\eta dS, \quad P_z = \int\rho\zeta dS$$

$$\begin{bmatrix}\mu\nu\\\alpha\end{bmatrix} = g_{\alpha\beta}\Gamma^\beta_{\mu\nu}$$

$$\frac{dP_x}{dt} = \int\rho u_x dS, \quad \frac{dP_y}{dt} = \int\rho u_y dS, \quad \frac{dP_z}{dt} = \int$$

$$u_\xi = \frac{u_x - v}{1 - u_x v/c^2}$$

$$u_\eta = \frac{u_y}{\beta(1 - u_x v/c^2)}$$

$$\int K_1 dx_1 dx_2 dx_3 = \int \frac{\partial T_{14}}{\partial x_4} dx_1 d.$$

$$u_\zeta = \frac{u_z}{\beta(1 - u_x v/c^2)},$$

$$\begin{bmatrix}\mu\nu\\\alpha\end{bmatrix} = g_{\alpha\beta}\Gamma^\beta_{\mu\nu}$$

$$\rho' = \frac{\partial X'}{\partial\xi} + \frac{\partial Y'}{\partial\eta} + \frac{\partial Z'}{\partial\zeta}$$

$$= \beta(1 - u_x v/c^2)\rho.$$

Perfection of means and confusion of aims seems, in my opinion, to characterize our age.

In order to be an immaculate member of a flock of sheep, one must above all be a sheep oneself.

It is easier to denature plutonium than it is to denature the evil spirit of man.

All our lauded technological progress—our very civilization—is like the ax in the hand of the pathological criminal.

The discovery of nuclear chain reactions need not bring about the destruction of mankind, any more than did the discovery of matches.

Conviction is a good mainspring, but a bad regulator.

As a human being, one has been endowed with just enough intelligence to be able to see clearly how utterly inadequate that intelligence is when confronted with what exists.

It is still the best to concern oneself with eternals, for from them alone flows the spirit that can restore peace and serenity to the world of humans.

In Nature, the overall principles represent a higher reality than does the single object.

Measured objectively, what a man can wrest from Truth by passionate striving is utterly infinitesimal. But the striving frees us from the bonds of the self and makes us comrades of those who are the best and the greatest.

There has been an earth for a little more than a billion years. As for the end of it I advise: Wait and see!

I am reminded of the German proverb: Everyone measures according to his own shoes.

We never cease to stand like curious children before the great Mystery into which we are born.

The man who regards his own life and that of his fellow creatures as meaningless is not merely unhappy but hardly fit for life.

Man grows cold faster than the planet he inhabits.

Small is the number of them that see with their own eyes and feel with their own hearts.

Joy in looking and comprehending is nature's most beautiful gift.

Einstein

Whoever undertakes to set himself up as judge in the field of truth and knowledge is shipwrecked by the laughter of the gods.

I want to know God's thoughts...all the rest are details.

No problem can be solved from the same consciousness that created it.

Great spirits have always encountered violent opposition from mediocre minds.

The most beautiful thing we can experience is the mysterious. It is the source of all true art and science.

Only two things are infinite, the universe and human stupidity, and I'm not sure about the former.

Imagination is more important than knowledge. Knowledge is limited. Imagination encircles the world.

The ideals which have always shone before me and filled me with the joy of living are goodness, beauty, and truth. To make a goal of comfort or happiness has never appealed to me; a system of ethics built on this basis would be sufficient only for a herd of cattle.

Man tries to make for himself in the fashion that suits him best an amplified and intelligible picture of the world; he then tries to some extent to substitute this cosmos of his for the world of experience, and thus to overcome it. This is what the painter, the poet, the speculative philosopher, and the natural scientists do, each in his own fashion. Each makes this cosmos and its construction the pivot of his emotional life, in order to find in this way peace and security which he cannot find in the narrow whirlpool of personal experience.

E i n s t e i n

Small is the number of them that see with their own eyes and feel with their own hearts.

Great spirits have often encountered violent opposition from mediocre minds.

We cannot despair of humanity, since we are ourselves human beings.

The fate of the world will be such as the world deserves.

That little word "we" I mistrust, and here's why:
No man of another can say "he" is "I."
Behind all agreement lies something amiss.
All seeming accord cloaks a lurking abyss.

Philosophy is like a mother who gave birth to and endowed all the other sciences. Therefore one should not scorn her in her nakedness and poverty, but should hope, rather, that part of her Don Quixote ideal will live on in her children so that they do not sink into philistinism.

Strange is our situation here upon earth.

The fairest thing we can experience is the mysterious. It is the fundamental emotion which stands at the cradle of true art and true science. He who knows it not and can no longer wonder, no longer feel amazement, is as good as dead, a snuffed-out candle.

Since I do not foresee that atomic energy is to be a great boon for a long time, I have to say that for the present it is a menace. Perhaps it is well that it should be. It may intimidate the human race to bring order into its international affairs, which, without the pressure of fear, it undoubtedly would not do.

It is difficult even to attach a precise meaning to the term "scientific truth." "Religious truth" conveys nothing clear to me at all.

Einstein

The pursuit of knowledge for its own sake, an almost fanatical love of justice, and the desire for personal independence—these are the features of the Jewish tradition which make me thank my lucky stars that I belong to it.

In the philosophical sense there is, in my opinion, no specifically Jewish point of view.

Thought is an end in itself, like music.

A butterfly is not a mole; but that is not something any butterfly should regret.

Every man has his own cosmology and who can say that his own theory is right.

I believe in the brotherhood of man and the uniqueness of the individual. But if you ask me to prove what I believe, I can't. You know them to be true but you could spend a whole lifetime without being able to prove them. There comes a point where the mind takes a higher plane of knowledge, but can never prove how it got there. All great discoveries have involved such a leap.

The deeper we search, the more we find there is to know, and as long as human life exists I believe that it will always be so.

Einstein

ON POLITICS

$$\mathbf{G} = \frac{1}{c}\int [\mathbf{D} \cdot \mathbf{H}]dS$$

$$\delta g_{\mu\nu} = g_{\mu\nu}\delta\rho, \quad \delta\phi_\mu = \frac{?}{?}$$

$$G_x = \frac{1}{c}\int (D_y H_z - D_z H_y)\,dS$$

$$\frac{d\phi}{ds} = \frac{\partial\phi}{\partial x_\mu}\frac{dx_\mu}{ds}$$

$$\mathbf{F}(\Sigma) = \left(l^2, \frac{l^2}{\beta}, \frac{l^2}{\beta}\right)$$

$$\psi = \frac{\partial\phi}{\partial x_\mu}\frac{dx_\mu}{ds}$$

$$\frac{\partial w^\mu}{\partial x_\mu} \equiv \mathfrak{W}_\mu^\mu$$

$$\frac{\partial\mathfrak{W}_\nu^\mu}{\partial x_\mu} - \Gamma_{\nu\beta}^\alpha\mathfrak{W}_\alpha^\beta \equiv$$

$$\xi + \frac{\beta(r'_0 - r')}{lc} = \beta^2\frac{v\xi}{c^2} + \frac{\beta}{lc}\left(\xi\frac{\partial r'}{\partial x} + \eta\frac{\partial r'}{\partial y} + \zeta\frac{\partial r'}{\partial z}\right)$$

$$\frac{\partial^2\gamma_{\mu\nu}}{\partial x_\alpha^2} = 2\kappa T_{\mu\nu}^*$$

$$A_\mu = \frac{\partial\phi}{\partial x_\mu}$$

$$P_x = \int\rho\xi dS, \quad P_y = \int\rho\eta dS, \quad P_z = \int\rho\zeta dS$$

$$\begin{bmatrix}\mu\nu\\\alpha\end{bmatrix} = g_{\alpha\beta}\Gamma_{\mu\nu}^\beta$$

$$\frac{dP_x}{dt} = \int\rho u_x dS, \quad \frac{dP_y}{dt} = \int\rho u_y dS, \quad \frac{dP_z}{dt} =$$

$$u_\xi = \frac{u_x - v}{1 - u_x v/c^2}$$

$$u_\eta = \frac{u_y}{\beta(1 - u_x v/c^2)}$$

$$\int K_1 dx_1 dx_2 dx_3 = \int \frac{\partial T_{14}}{\partial x_4}\,dx_1 c$$

$$u_\zeta = \frac{u_z}{\beta(1 - u_x v/c^2)},$$

$$\begin{bmatrix}\mu\nu\\\alpha\end{bmatrix} = g_{\alpha\beta}\Gamma_{\mu\nu}^\beta$$

$$\rho' = \frac{\partial X'}{\partial\xi} + \frac{\partial Y'}{\partial\eta} + \frac{\partial Z'}{\partial\zeta}$$
$$= \beta(1 - u_x v/c^2)\rho.$$

$$\frac{\beta^2}{c^2}\frac{v\xi}{?} + \frac{\beta(r'_0 - r')}{lc} = \beta^2\frac{v\xi}{c^2} + \frac{\beta}{lc}\left(\xi\frac{\partial r'}{\partial x} + \eta\frac{\partial r'}{\partial y} + \zeta\frac{\partial r'}{\partial z}\right)$$

Political leaders or governments owe their position partly to force and partly to popular election. They cannot be regarded as representative of the best elements, morally or intellectually, in their respective nations.

To tolerate parleying with the worst enemies of civilization: there is a kind of compliance which is a crime against humanity—though it passes for political wisdom.

In these days of democratic government the fate of nations hangs on the people themselves; each individual must always bear that in mind.

The prestige of government has undoubtedly been lowered considerably by the Prohibition law. For nothing is more destructive of respect for the government and the law of the land than passing laws which cannot be enforced. It is an open secret that the dangerous increase of crime in this country is closely connected with this.

I regard it as the chief duty of the state to protect the individual and give him the opportunity to develop into a creative personality.

The greatest obstacle to international order is that monstrously exaggerated spirit of nationalism which also goes by the fair-sounding but misused name of patriotism.

In my opinion, it is not right to bring politics into scientific matters, nor should individuals be held responsible for the government of the country to which they happen to belong.

My political ideal is democracy.

The led must not be coerced, they must be able to choose their leader. I believe it to be an invariable rule that tyrants of genius are succeeded by scoundrels.

An autocratic system of coercion, in my opinion, soon degenerates. For force always attracts men of low morality.

Let me begin with a confession of political faith: The state is made for man, not man for the state.

Nationalism is an infantile sickness. It is the measles of the human race.

Politics is a pendulum whose swings between anarchy and tyranny are fueled by perennially rejuvenated illusions.

Although I am a convinced democrat I know well that the human community would stagnate and even degenerate without a minority of socially conscious and upright men and women willing to make sacrifices for their convictions.

The old problem of what should be done to give the power into the hands of capable and well-meaning persons has so far resisted all efforts.

As long as I have any choice, I will only stay in a country where political liberty, tolerance, and equality of all citizens before the law prevail.

E i n s t e i n

Being tolerant does not mean being indifferent towards the actions and feelings of others.Understanding and empathy must also be present, the most important kind of tolerance is of the individual by society and the state.

Any government is certain to be evil to some extent.

Only a free individual can make a discovery.

We should not make the mistake of blaming capitalism for all existing social and political evils.

In a healthy nation there is a kind of dynamic balance between the will of the people and the government which prevents its degeneration into tyranny.

We must overcome the horrible obstacles of national frontiers.

The state has become a modern idol whose suggestive power few men are able to escape.

Taken on the whole, I would believe that Gandhi's views were the most enlightened of all the political men in our time.

Anti-Semitism has always been the cheapest means employed by selfish minorities for deceiving the people.

My ideal remains the settlement of all international dispute by arbitration.

Give heed to your clever and patriotic womenfolk and remember that the Capitol of mighty Rome was once saved by the cackling of its faithful geese.

Einstein

ON RELIGION

$$G = \frac{1}{c}\int [\mathbf{D} \cdot \mathbf{H}]dS$$

$$\delta g_{\mu\nu} = g_{\mu\nu}\delta\rho, \quad \delta\phi_\mu = \frac{\partial}{}$$

$$G_x = \frac{1}{c}\int (D_y H_z - D_z H_y)dS$$

$$\frac{d\phi}{ds} = \frac{\partial\phi}{\partial x_\mu}\frac{dx_\mu}{ds} \qquad F(\Sigma) = \left(l^2, \frac{l^2}{\beta}, \frac{l^2}{\beta}\right)F$$

$$\psi = \frac{\partial\phi}{\partial x_\mu}\frac{dx_\mu}{ds} \qquad \frac{\partial w^\mu}{\partial x_\mu} \equiv \mathfrak{W}^\mu_\mu$$

$$\frac{\partial \mathfrak{W}^\mu_\nu}{\partial x_\mu} - \Gamma^\alpha_{\nu\beta}\mathfrak{W}^\beta_\alpha \equiv$$

$$+ \frac{\beta(r'_0 - r')}{lc} = \beta^2\frac{v\xi}{c^2} + \frac{\beta}{lc}\left(\xi\frac{\partial r'}{\partial x} + \eta\frac{\partial r'}{\partial y} + \zeta\frac{\partial r'}{\partial z}\right)$$

$$A_\mu = \frac{\partial\phi}{\partial x_\mu}$$

$$\frac{\partial^2\gamma_{\mu\nu}}{\partial x_\alpha^2} = 2\kappa T^*_{\mu\nu}$$

$$P_x = \int\rho\xi dS, \quad P_y = \int\rho\eta dS, \quad P_z = \int\rho\zeta dS$$

$$\left[{}^{\mu\nu}_\alpha\right] = g_{\alpha\beta}\Gamma^\beta_{\mu\nu}$$

$$\frac{dP_x}{dt} = \int\rho u_x dS, \quad \frac{dP_y}{dt} = \int\rho u_y dS, \quad \frac{dP_z}{dt} = \int$$

$$u_\xi = \frac{u_x - v}{1 - u_x v/c^2}$$

$$u_\eta = \frac{u_y}{\beta(1 - u_x v/c^2)} \qquad \int K_1 dx_1 dx_2 dx_3 = \int\frac{\partial T_{14}}{\partial x_4}dx_1 dx$$

$$u_\zeta = \frac{u_z}{\beta(1 - u_x v/c^2)},$$

$$\left[{}^{\mu\nu}_\alpha\right] = g_{\alpha\beta}\Gamma^\beta_{\mu\nu}$$

$$\rho' = \frac{\partial X'}{\partial\xi} + \frac{\partial Y'}{\partial\eta} + \frac{\partial Z'}{\partial\zeta}$$

$$= \beta(1 - u_x v/c^2)\rho.$$

I do not believe in a personal God and I have never denied this but have expressed it clearly. If something is in me which can be called religious then it is the unbounded admiration for the structure of the world so far as our science can reveal it.

To the sphere of religion belongs the faith that the regulations valid for the world of existence are rational, that it is comprehensible to reason. I cannot conceive of a genuine scientist without that profound faith.

Subtle is the Lord, but malicious He is not.

The main source of the present-day conflicts between the spheres of religion and of science lies in this concept of a personal God.

Since our inner experiences consist of reproductions and combinations of sensory impressions, the concept of a soul without a body seems to be empty and devoid of meaning.

What humanity owes to personalities like Buddha, Moses, and Jesus ranks for me higher than all the achievements of the inquiring and constructive mind.

The further the spiritual evolution of mankind advances, the more certain it seems to me that the path to genuine religiosity does not lie through the fear of life and the fear of death, and blind faith, but through striving after rational knowledge. In this sense I believe that the priest must become a teacher if he wishes to do justice to his lofty educational mission.

God does not play dice with the universe.

Science without religion is lame, religion without science is blind.

The Jews are a community bound together by ties of blood and tradition, and not of religion only: the attitude of the rest of the world toward them is sufficient proof of this.

A belief bound up with deep feeling, in a superior mind that reveals itself in the world of experience, represents my conception of God.

Before God we are equally wise—and equally foolish.

If one purges the Judaism of the Prophets and Christianity as Jesus Christ taught it of all subsequent additions especially those of the priests, one is left with a teaching which is capable of curing all the social ills of humanity.

All men dance to the tune of an invisible piper.

I feel such solidarity with all living people that it is a matter of indifference to me where the individual begins and where he ceases.

I really don't know enough about my religious feelings. I have always known exactly what I should do, and I feel satisfied with that.

Einstein

If I were not a Jew I would be a Quaker.

I cannot accept any concept of God based on the fear of life or the fear of death or blind faith. I cannot prove to you that there is no personal God, but if I were to speak of him I would be a liar.

ON SCIENCE

$$G = \frac{1}{c}\int [\mathbf{D} \cdot \mathbf{H}]dS$$

$$\delta g_{\mu\nu} = g_{\mu\nu}\delta\rho, \quad \delta\phi_\mu =$$

$$G_x = \frac{1}{c}\int (D_y H_z - D_z H_y)dS$$

$$\frac{d\phi}{ds} = \frac{\partial\phi}{\partial x_\mu}\frac{dx_\mu}{ds}$$

$$\mathbf{F}(\Sigma) = \left(l^2, \frac{l^2}{\beta}, \frac{l^2}{\beta}\right)$$

$$\psi = \frac{\partial\phi}{\partial x_\mu}\frac{dx_\mu}{ds}$$

$$\frac{\partial w^\mu}{\partial x_\mu} \equiv \mathfrak{W}^\mu_\mu$$

$$\frac{\partial \mathfrak{W}^\mu_\nu}{\partial x_\mu} - \Gamma^\alpha_{\nu\beta}\mathfrak{W}^\beta_\alpha =$$

$$\frac{\xi}{2} + \frac{\beta(r'_0 - r')}{lc} = \beta^2\frac{v\xi}{c^2} + \frac{\beta}{lc}\left(\xi\frac{\partial r'}{\partial x} + \eta\frac{\partial r'}{\partial y} + \zeta\frac{\partial r'}{\partial z}\right)$$

$$A_\mu = \frac{\partial\phi}{\partial x_\mu}$$

$$\frac{\partial^2\gamma_{\mu\nu}}{\partial x_\alpha^2} = 2\kappa T^*_{\mu\nu}$$

$$P_x = \int\rho\xi dS, \quad P_y = \int\rho\eta dS, \quad P_z = \int\rho\zeta dS$$

$$[^{\mu\nu}_\alpha] = g_{\alpha\beta}\Gamma^\beta_{\mu\nu}$$

$$\frac{dP_x}{dt} = \int\rho u_x dS, \quad \frac{dP_y}{dt} = \int\rho u_y dS, \quad \frac{dP_z}{dt} =$$

$$u_\xi = \frac{u_x - v}{1 - u_x v/c^2}$$

$$u_\eta = \frac{u_y}{\beta(1 - u_x v/c^2)}$$

$$\int K_1 dx_1 dx_2 dx_3 = \int \frac{\partial T_{14}}{\partial x_4}dx_1$$

$$u_\zeta = \frac{u_z}{\beta(1 - u_x v/c^2)},$$

$$[^{\mu\nu}_\alpha] = g_{\alpha\beta}\Gamma^\beta_{\mu\nu}$$

$$\rho' = \frac{\partial X'}{\partial\xi} + \frac{\partial Y'}{\partial\eta} + \frac{\partial Z'}{\partial\zeta}$$
$$= \beta(1 - u_x v/c^2)\rho.$$

Mathematics are all well and good but Nature keeps dragging us around by the nose.

When the solution is simple, God is answering.

The most incomprehensible thing about the world is that it is comprehensible.

The important thing is not to stop questioning.

As far as the laws of mathematics refer to reality, they are not certain; and as far as they are certain, they do not refer to reality.

One reason why mathematics enjoys special esteem, above all other sciences, is that its laws are absolutely certain and indisputable, while those of all other sciences are to some extent debatable and in constant danger of being overthrown by newly discovered facts.

What physics looks for: the simplest possible system of thought which will bind together the observed facts.

I have little patience with scientists who take a board of wood, look for its thinnest part, and drill a great number of holes where drilling is easy.

Science is a wonderful thing if one does not have to earn one's living at it. Only when we do not have to be accountable to anybody can we find joy in scientific endeavor.

The problem of gravitation converted me into a believing rationalist, that is, into someone who searches for the only reliable source of Truth in mathematical simplicity.

The more one chases after quanta, the better they hide themselves.

When I have no special problem to occupy my mind, I love to reconstruct proofs of mathematical and physical theorems that have long been known to me. There is no goal in this, merely an opportunity to indulge in the pleasant occupation of thinking.

The scientific theorist is not to be envied. For Nature, or more precisely experiment, is an inexorable and not very friendly judge of his work. It never says "Yes" to a theory. In the most favorable cases it says "Maybe," and in the great majority of cases simply "No." If an experiment agrees with a theory it means for the latter "Maybe," and if it does not agree it means "No." Probably every theory will some day experience its "No"—most theories, soon after conception.

Knowledge exists in two forms—lifeless, stored in books, and alive in the consciousness of men. The second form of existence is after all the essential one; the first, indispensable as it may be, occupies only an inferior position.

E i n s t e i n

I am not involved, thank God, and no longer need to take part in the competition of the big brains. Participating in it has always seemed to me to be an awful type of slavery no less evil than the passion for money or power.

Body and soul are not two different things, but only two different ways of perceiving the same thing. Similarly, physics and psychology are only different attempts to link our experiences together by way of systematic thought.

The most beautiful experience we can have is the mysterious; it is the fundamental emotion which stands at the cradle of true art and true science.

Things should be made as simple as possible, but not any simpler.

> *Watch the stars, and from them learn*
> *To the Master's honor all must turn*
> *Each in its track, without a sound*
> *Forever tracing Newton's ground.*

Put your hand on a hot stove for a minute, and it seems like an hour. Sit with a pretty girl for an hour, and it seems like a minute. That's relativity.

Where the world ceases to be the scene of our personal hopes and wishes, where we face it as free beings admiring, asking, and observing, there we enter the realm of Art and Science.

Newton, Faraday, and Maxwell put physics on a new basis: the theory of relativity may indeed be said to have put a sort of finishing touch to the mighty intellectual edifice of Maxwell and Lorentz, inasmuch as it seeks to extend field physics to all phenomena, gravitation included.

If you want to find out anything from the theoretical physicists about the methods they use, I advise you to stick closely to one principle: Don't listen to their words, fix your attention on their deeds.

Einstein

The whole of science is nothing more than a refinement of everyday thinking.

I'm not much with people and I'm not a family man. I want my peace. I want to know how God created this world. I am not interested in this or that phenomenon, in the spectrum of this or that element. I want to know His thoughts, the rest are details.

Since the mathematicians have attacked the relativity theory, I myself no longer understand it any more.

The distinction between past, present, and future is only an illusion, however persistent.

Only a monomaniac gets what we commonly refer to as results.

The nonmathematician is seized by a mysterious shuddering when he hears of 'four-dimensional' things, by a feeling not unlike that awakened by thoughts of the occult. And yet there is no more commonplace statement than that the world in which we live is a four-dimensional space-time continuum.

Unthinking respect for authority is the greatest enemy of truth.

Possibly we shall one day know a little more than we do now. But the real nature of things, that we shall never know, never.

When the blind beetle crawls over the surface of a globe, he doesn't notice that the track he has covered is curved. I was lucky enough to have spotted it.

Space is not merely a background for events, but possesses an autonomous structure.

Mysticism is in fact the only reproach that people cannot level at my theory (of relativity).

Einstein

For the rest of my life I want to reflect on what light is.

It was formerly believed that if all material things disappeared out of the universe, time and space would be left. According to the relativity theory, however, time and space disappear together with the things.

All physical theories, their mathematical expressions apart, ought to lend themselves to so simple a description that "even a child could understand them."

We know nothing about it all. All our knowledge is but the knowledge of schoolchildren.

I am anxious to draw attention to the fact that this theory is not speculative in origin. It owes its invention entirely to the desire to make physical theory fit observed facts as well as possible. We have here no revolutionary act, but the natural combination of a line that can be traced through centuries. The abandon-ment of certain notions connected with space, time, and motion, hitherto treated as fundamentals, must not be regarded as arbitrary, but only as conditioned by observed facts.

Splitting the atom by bombardment is like shooting at birds in the dark in a region where there are few birds.

It is the duty of a scientist to remain obscure.

Einstein

ON SOCIAL MATTERS

$$\mathbf{G} = \frac{1}{c}\int[\mathbf{D}\cdot\mathbf{H}]dS$$

$$\delta g_{\mu\nu} = g_{\mu\nu}\delta\rho, \quad \delta\phi_\mu = \frac{\partial}{}$$

$$G_x = \frac{1}{c}\int(D_y H_z - D_z H_y)dS$$

$$\frac{d\phi}{ds} = \frac{\partial\phi}{\partial x_\mu}\frac{dx_\mu}{ds}$$

$$\mathbf{F}(\Sigma) = \left(l^2, \frac{l^2}{\beta}, \frac{l^2}{\beta}\right)$$

$$\psi = \frac{\partial\phi}{\partial x_\mu}\frac{dx_\mu}{ds}$$

$$\frac{\partial w^\mu}{\partial x_\mu} \equiv \mathfrak{W}^\mu_\mu$$

$$\frac{\partial\mathfrak{W}^\mu_\nu}{\partial x_\mu} - \Gamma^\alpha_{\nu\beta}\mathfrak{W}^\beta_\alpha \equiv$$

$$\xi + \frac{\beta(r'_0 - r')}{lc} = \beta^2\frac{v\xi}{c^2} + \frac{\beta}{lc}\left(\xi\frac{\partial r'}{\partial x} + \eta\frac{\partial r'}{\partial y} + \zeta\frac{\partial r'}{\partial z}\right)$$

$$A_\mu = \frac{\partial\phi}{\partial x_\mu}$$

$$\frac{\partial^2\gamma_{\mu\nu}}{\partial x_\alpha^2} = 2\kappa T^*_{\mu\nu}$$

$$P_x = \int\rho\xi dS, \quad P_y = \int\rho\eta dS, \quad P_z = \int\rho\zeta dS$$

$$\begin{bmatrix}\mu\nu\\\alpha\end{bmatrix} = g_{\alpha\beta}\Gamma^\beta_{\mu\nu}$$

$$\frac{dP_x}{dt} = \int\rho u_x dS, \quad \frac{dP_y}{dt} = \int\rho u_y dS, \quad \frac{dP_z}{dt} = \int$$

$$u_\xi = \frac{u_x - v}{1 - u_x v/c^2}$$

$$u_\eta = \frac{u_y}{\beta(1 - u_x v/c^2)}$$

$$\int K_1 dx_1 dx_2 dx_3 = \int\frac{\partial T_{14}}{\partial x_4}dx_1 d$$

$$u_\zeta = \frac{u_z}{\beta(1 - u_x v/c^2)},$$

$$\begin{bmatrix}\mu\nu\\\alpha\end{bmatrix} = g_{\alpha\beta}\Gamma^\beta_{\mu\nu}$$

$$\rho' = \frac{\partial X'}{\partial\xi} + \frac{\partial Y'}{\partial\eta} + \frac{\partial Z'}{\partial\zeta}$$

$$= \beta(1 - u_x v/c^2)\rho.$$

People are all the same.

The introduction of compulsory military service is, to my mind, the prime cause of the moral decay of the white race.

Man is, at one and the same time, a solitary being and a social being.

By painful experience we have learned that rational thinking does not suffice to solve the problems of our social life.

We are all nourished and housed by the work of our fellow men and we have to pay honestly for it, not only by work chosen for the sake of our inner satisfaction but by work which, according to general opinion, serves them. Otherwise one becomes a parasite however modest our wants might be.

You ask me what I think about war and the death penalty. The latter question is simpler. I am against it only because I do not trust people, that is, the courts.

Those who would preserve the spirit must also look after the body to which it is attached.

When, in the mornings, I become nauseated by the news that the *New York Times* sets before us, I always reflect that it is anyway better than the Hitlerism that we only barely managed to finish off.

I am only coming to Princeton to do research, not to teach. There is too much education altogether, especially in American schools. The only rational way of educating is to be an example—if one can't help it, a warning example.

How wretchedly inadequate is the theoretical physicist as he stands before Nature—and his students!

Study and, in general, the pursuit of truth and beauty is a sphere of activity in which we are permitted to remain children all our lives.

One cannot learn anything so well as by experiencing it oneself.

[On being asked what ideal qualities the trustees should seek in a director of The Institute for Advanced Study]: You should look for a very quiet man who will not disturb people who are trying to think.

The gentlemen in Berlin are gambling on me as if I were a prize hen. As for myself I don't even know whether I'm going to lay another egg.

A good joke should not be repeated too often.

Einstein

Personally I consider it indecent to delve into people's private affairs, and the world would certainly fare better if newspapers cared more for things that really matter instead of dealing with trifles.

The development of general ability for independent thinking and judgment should always be placed foremost, not the acquisition of special knowledge.

Words are and remain an empty sound, and the road to perdition has ever been accomplished by lip service to an ideal. But personalities are not formed by what is heard and said, but by labor and activity. The most important method of education accordingly always has consisted of that in which the pupil was urged to actual performance.

To me, the worst thing seems to be for a school principally to work with methods of fear, force, and artificial authority. Give into the power of the teacher and the fewest possible coercive measures, so that the only source of the pupil's respect for the teacher is the human and intellectual qualities of the latter.

The school has always been the most important means of transferring the wealth of tradition from one generation to the next. This applies today in an even higher degree than in former times, for through modern development of the economic life, the family as bearer of tradition and education has been weakened. The continuance and health of human society is therefore in a still higher degree dependent on the school than formerly.

It is the supreme art of the teacher to awaken joy in creative expression and knowledge.

Teaching should be such that what is offered is perceived as a valuable gift and not as a hard duty.

Einstein

In schools: should language predominate or technical education in science? To this I answer: it is of secondary importance. If a young person has trained his muscles and physical endurance by gymnastics and walking, he will later be fitted or every physical work. This is also analogous to the training of the mind and the exercising of the mental and manual skill.

Wisdom is not a product of schooling but of the life-long attempt to acquire it.

In the schools, history could be used as a means of interpreting progress in civilization and not of inculcating ideals of imperialistic power and military success. Finally, it is at least of indirect importance that in geography, as well as in history, a sympathetic understanding of the characteristics of various peoples be stimulated and this understanding should include those peoples designated as "primitive" or "backward."

It is not enough to teach a man a specialty. Through it he may become a kind of useful machine but not a harmoniously developed personality. It is essential that the student acquire an understanding of and a lively feeling for values. He must acquire a vivid sense of the beautiful and of the morally good. Otherwise he—with his specialized knowledge—more closely resembles a well-trained dog than a harmoniously developed person.

In the past it never occurred to me that every casual remark of mine would be snatched up and recorded, otherwise I would have crept further into my shell.

It is not my fault that laymen obtain an exaggerated impression of the significance of my efforts. Rather, this is due to writers of popular science and in particular to newspaper correspondents who present everything as sensationally as possible.

Einstein

Somebody who reads only newspapers and at best books of contemporary authors looks to me like an extremely nearsighted man who scorns eyeglasses. He is completely dependent on the prejudices and fashions of his times, since he never gets to see or hear anything else.

ON WAR AND PEACE

$$G = \frac{1}{c}\int [\mathbf{D} \cdot \mathbf{H}]dS$$

$$\delta g_{\mu\nu} = g_{\mu\nu}\delta\rho, \quad \delta\phi_\mu = \frac{\partial}{\tau}$$

$$G_x = \frac{1}{c}\int (D_y H_\varepsilon - D_z H_y)dS$$

$$\frac{d\phi}{ds} = \frac{\partial\phi}{\partial x_\mu}\frac{dx_\mu}{ds}$$

$$F(\Sigma) = \left(l^2, \frac{l^2}{\bar\beta}, \frac{l^2}{\beta} \right) F$$

$$\psi = \frac{\partial\phi}{dx_\mu}\frac{dx_\mu}{ds}$$

$$\frac{\partial w^\mu}{\partial x_\mu} \equiv \mathfrak{W}^\mu_\mu$$

$$\frac{\partial\mathfrak{W}^\mu_\nu}{\partial x_\mu} - \Gamma^\alpha_{\nu\beta}\mathfrak{W}^\beta_\alpha \equiv$$

$$+ \frac{\beta(r'_0 - r')}{lc} = \beta^2\frac{v\xi}{c^2} + \frac{\beta}{lc}\left(\xi\frac{\partial r'}{\partial x} + \eta\frac{\partial r'}{\partial y} + \zeta\frac{\partial r'}{\partial z} \right)$$

$$A_\mu = \frac{\partial\phi}{\partial x_\mu}$$

$$\frac{\partial^2\gamma_{\mu\nu}}{\partial x_\alpha^2} = 2\kappa T^*_{\mu\nu}$$

$$P_x = \int\rho\xi dS, \quad P_y = \int\rho\eta dS, \quad P_z = \int\rho\zeta dS$$

$$[^{\mu\nu}_\alpha] = g_{\alpha\beta}\Gamma^\beta_{\mu\nu}$$

$$\frac{dP_x}{dt} = \int\rho u_x dS, \quad \frac{dP_y}{dt} = \int\rho u_y dS, \quad \frac{dP_z}{dt} = \int\rho$$

$$u_\xi = \frac{u_x - v}{1 - u_x v/c^2}$$

$$u_\eta = \frac{u_y}{\beta(1 - u_x v/c^2)}$$

$$\int K_1 dx_1 dx_2 dx_3 = \int \frac{\partial T_{14}}{\partial x_4} dx_1 dx$$

$$u_\zeta = \frac{u_z}{\beta(1 - u_x v/c^2)},$$

$$[^{\mu\nu}_\alpha] = g_{\alpha\beta}\Gamma^\beta_{\mu\nu}$$

$$\rho' = \frac{\partial X'}{\partial\xi} + \frac{\partial Y'}{\partial\eta} + \frac{\partial Z'}{\partial\zeta}$$

$$= \beta(1 - u_x v/c^2)\rho.$$

This topic brings me to that worst outcrop of herd life, the military system, which I abhor. That a man can take pleasure in marching in fours to the strains of a band is enough to make me despise him. He has only been given his big brain by mistake; unprotected spinal marrow was all he needed.

The only defense a minority has is passive resistance.

While I am a convinced pacifist there are circumstances in which I believe the use of force is appropriate— namely, in the face of an enemy unconditionally bent on destroying me and my people.

You ask me what I thought when I heard that the Potsdam police had invaded my summer home to search for hidden weapons: What else would a Nazi policeman assume?

Violence sometimes may have cleared away obstructions quickly, but it never has proved itself creative.

How will World War III be fought? I do not know; but I do know how World War IV will be—with sticks and stones.

This disgrace to civilization [war] should be done away with at once. Heroism at command, senseless brutality, deplorable love-of-country stance, how violently I hate all this, how despicable and ignoble war is; I would rather be torn to shreds than be a part of so base an action!

.

It is my conviction that killing under the cloak of war is nothing but an act of murder.

Peace cannot be achieved through violence, it can only be attained through understanding.

The release of atomic energy has not created a new problem. It has merely made more urgent the necessity of solving an existing one. What has been changed is the destructiveness of war.

War is not a parlor game in which the players obediently stick to the rules. Where life and death are at stake, rules and obligations go by the board.

May the conscience and the common sense of the peoples be awakened so that we may reach a new stage in the life of nations, where people will look back on war as an incomprehensible aberration of their forefathers.

Whether we find the way of peace or continue along the old road of brute force, so unworthy of our civilization, depends on ourselves. On the one side the freedom of the individual and the security of society beckon to us; on the other slavery for the individual and the annihilation of our civilization threaten us. Our fate will be according to our deserts.

People will not disarm step by step; they will disarm at one blow or not at all.

Einstein

The armament industry is indeed one of the greatest dangers that beset mankind. It is the hidden evil power.

A pacifism which does not actively fight against the armament of nations is and must remain impotent.

If the workers of this world, men and women, decide not to manufacture and transport ammunition, it would end war for all time. We must do that. Dedicate our lives to drying up the source of war: ammunition factories.

War cannot be humanized, it can only be abolished.

Even if only 2 percent of those assigned to perform military service should announce their refusal to fight, governments would be powerless, they would not dare send such a large number of people to jail.

ABOUT ALBERT EINSTEIN

$$\mathbf{G} = \frac{1}{c}\int [\mathbf{D} \cdot \mathbf{H}]dS$$

$$\delta g_{\mu\nu} = g_{\mu\nu}\delta\rho, \quad \delta\phi_\mu = \frac{\partial\phi}{2}$$

$$\mathbf{G}_x = \frac{1}{c}\int (\mathbf{D}_y\mathbf{H}_z - \mathbf{D}_z\mathbf{H}_y)dS$$

$$\frac{d\phi}{ds} = \frac{\partial\phi}{\partial x_\mu}\frac{dx_\mu}{ds}$$

$$\mathbf{F}(\Sigma) = \left(l^2, \frac{l^2}{\beta}, \frac{l^2}{\beta}\right)\mathbf{F}$$

$$\psi = \frac{\partial\phi}{\partial x_\mu}\frac{dx_\mu}{ds}$$

$$\frac{\partial w^\mu}{\partial x_\mu} \equiv \mathfrak{W}^\mu_\mu$$

$$\frac{\partial\mathfrak{W}^\mu_\nu}{\partial x_\mu} - \Gamma^\alpha_{\nu\beta}\mathfrak{W}^\beta_\alpha \equiv$$

$$+ \frac{\beta(r'_0 - r)}{lc} = \beta^2\frac{v\xi}{c^2} + \frac{\beta}{lc}\left(\xi\frac{\partial r'}{\partial x} + \eta\frac{\partial r'}{\partial y} + \zeta\frac{\partial r'}{\partial z}\right)$$

$$\mathbf{A}_\mu = \frac{\partial\phi}{\partial x_\mu}$$

$$\frac{\partial^2\gamma_{\mu\nu}}{\partial x_\alpha{}^2} = 2\kappa T^*_{\mu\nu}$$

$$\mathbf{P}_x = \int\rho\xi dS, \quad \mathbf{P}_y = \int\rho\eta dS, \quad \mathbf{P}_z = \int\rho\zeta dS$$

$$\begin{bmatrix}\mu\nu\\\alpha\end{bmatrix} = g_{\alpha\beta}\Gamma^\beta_{\mu\nu}$$

$$\frac{d\mathbf{P}_x}{dt} = \int\rho u_x dS, \quad \frac{d\mathbf{P}_y}{dt} = \int\rho u_y dS, \quad \frac{d\mathbf{P}_z}{dt} = \int$$

$$u_\xi = \frac{u_x - v}{1 - u_x v/c^2}$$

$$u_\eta = \frac{u_y}{\beta(1 - u_x v/c^2)}$$

$$\int K_1 dx_1 dx_2 dx_3 = \int \frac{\partial T_{14}}{\partial x_4}dx_1 dx$$

$$u_\zeta = \frac{u_z}{\beta(1 - u_x v/c^2)},$$

$$\begin{bmatrix}\mu\nu\\\alpha\end{bmatrix} = g_{\alpha\beta}\Gamma^\beta_{\mu\nu}$$

$$\rho' = \frac{\partial X'}{\partial\xi} + \frac{\partial Y'}{\partial\eta} + \frac{\partial Z'}{\partial\zeta}$$

$$= \beta(1 - u_x v/c^2)\rho.$$

ALBERT EINSTEIN was born in Ulm, Germany, on March 14, 1879. He lived as a boy in Munich and Milan and graduated from the Federal Institute of Technology in Zürich in 1900. From an early age he opposed German military and political views and became a resident of Switzerland in 1901. After graduating from the Federal Institute, he took a job at the Swiss Patent Office and pursued earning his doctorate in theoretical physics at the University of Zürich, graduating in 1905.

During 1905, which physicists and scholars call his "Miracle Year," he published papers in the *Annals of Physics* on light quanta, Brownian motion, special relativity (relativity without gravity), and inertia. His short paper, "Does Radiation Convey Inertia?", contains, in an almost off-the-cuff manner, the now famous formula $E=mc^2$ (Energy equals mass times the speed of light squared), which forms the basis for his theory of relativity.

In 1912 he became a professor at the German University in Prague. By 1913 he had won international fame and was invited by the Prussian Academy of Sciences to become a director of theoretical physics. In 1916 he published the *General Theory of Relativity*, which posited that the speed of light is the limiting speed of all bodies with mass, that mass and energy are equivalent, and that gravitation is a determiner of the curvature of a space-time continuum. He was awarded the 1921 Nobel Prize in physics for his research on the theory of the photoelectric effect.

In his pursuit of a unified theory of the universe at the atomic level, Einstein insisted that his theories and mathematical formulas have simplicity and beauty, qualities that he saw in the universe—and ultimately in the concept of God. He was a reluctant father of modern quantum physics, often in conflict with his fellow physicists over the theories of quantum mechanics, which stated that all events were the results of the destruction and creation of particles on the atomic level, and that these events were not precisely definable or predictable. Quantum mechanics was opposed to classical mechanics which stated that all properties were, in theory, definable by mathematical formula and therefore predictable.

After Einstein met fellow physicist Niels Bohr in 1920 to share ideas and philosophy, the pair entered into a lifelong argument as to whether, at its base, quantum dynamics did or did not demand the presence of a unifying force. The discussions led Einstein to argue that "God does not play dice with the universe."

In 1934, during Hitler's rise to power, he emigrated from Germany to the United States, settling in at the Princeton

Institute for Advanced Study and becoming an American citizen in 1940.

Ironically, although a lifelong pacifist, his early research had shown the theoretical possibility of an atomic weapon. The specter of Hitlerism and early Nazi research into an atomic bomb led him, in 1939, to sign a letter suggested by American physicists Leo Szilard and Edward Teller, to President Roosevelt. In the letter he argued for the importance of developing weapons that could counter the German threat. Although he was never involved directly in research and development of these weapons, his support of its necessity was vital to the formation of the Manhattan Project whose work led to the development of the atomic bomb.

Einstein struggled throughout his entire career to incorporate the idea of a unifying force into quantum physics, believing that without it the theory would be forever incomplete. In general, the scientific establishment felt he was on the wrong track. But times have changed. In 1979, at the Jerusalem Seminars held in honor of the centenary of his birth, quantum physicist Paul Dirac was quoted as saying, "I think it is very likely that in the long run, Einstein will turn out to be correct." As scientists continue to explore the sub-

Einstein

atomic world, data and theory lead them in the direction in which Einstein had so eloquently pointed.

He pursued his love of mathematics and science and continued his fight for, peace, sanity, and compassion until his death in Princeton, New Jersey, on April 15, 1955.

$$G = \frac{1}{c}\int [\mathbf{D}\cdot\mathbf{H}]dS$$

$$\delta g_{\mu\nu} = g_{\mu\nu}\delta\rho, \quad \delta\phi_\mu = \frac{\partial(\delta\rho)}{\partial x_\mu}$$

$$G_x = \frac{1}{c}\int (D_y H_z - D_z H_y)dS$$

$$\frac{d\phi}{ds} = \frac{\partial\phi}{\partial x_\mu}\frac{dx_\mu}{ds}$$

$$\mathbf{F}(\Sigma) = \left(l^2, \frac{l^2}{\beta}, \frac{l^2}{\beta}\right)\mathbf{F}(\Sigma'$$

$$\psi = \frac{\partial\phi}{\partial x_\mu}\frac{dx_\mu}{ds}$$

$$\frac{\partial w^\mu}{\partial x_\mu} \equiv \mathfrak{W}^\mu_\mu$$

$$\frac{\partial\mathfrak{W}^\mu_\nu}{\partial x_\mu} - \Gamma^\alpha_{\nu\beta}\mathfrak{W}^\beta_\alpha \equiv \tfrac{1}{2}\mathrm{F}$$

$$\frac{\beta(r'_0 - r')}{lc} = \beta^2\frac{v\xi}{c^2} + \frac{\beta}{lc}\left(\xi\frac{\partial r'}{\partial x} + \eta\frac{\partial r'}{\partial y} + \zeta\frac{\partial r'}{\partial z}\right)$$

$$A_\mu = \frac{\partial\phi}{\partial x_\mu}$$

$$\frac{\partial^2\gamma_{\mu\nu}}{\partial x_\alpha^2} = 2\kappa T^*_{\mu\nu}$$

$$P_x = \int\rho\xi dS, \quad P_y = \int\rho\eta dS, \quad P_z = \int\rho\zeta dS$$

$$[{}^{\mu\nu}_\alpha] = g_{\alpha\beta}\Gamma^\beta_{\mu\nu}$$

$$\frac{dP_x}{dt} = \int\rho u_x dS, \quad \frac{dP_y}{dt} = \int\rho u_y dS, \quad \frac{dP_z}{dt} = \int\rho u_z$$

$$u_\xi = \frac{u_x - v}{1 - u_x v/c^2}$$

$$u_\eta = \frac{u_y}{\beta(1 - u_x v/c^2)}$$

$$\int K_1 dx_1 dx_2 dx_3 = \int \frac{\partial T_{14}}{\partial x_4}dx_1 dx_2 d$$

$$u_\zeta = \frac{u_z}{\beta(1 - u_x v/c^2)},$$

$$-i\frac{?}{c}$$

$$[{}^{\mu\nu}_\alpha] = g_{\alpha\beta}\Gamma^\beta_{\mu\nu}$$

$$\rho' = \frac{\partial X'}{\partial\xi} + \frac{\partial Y'}{\partial\eta} + \frac{\partial Z'}{\partial\zeta}$$

$$= \beta(1 - u_x v/c^2)\rho.$$

$$\mathbf{G} = \frac{1}{c}\int[\mathbf{D}\cdot\mathbf{H}]dS$$

$$\delta g_{\mu\nu} = g_{\mu\nu}\delta\rho, \quad \delta\phi_\mu = \frac{\partial(\delta\rho)}{\partial x_\mu}$$

$$G_x = \frac{1}{c}\int(\mathrm{D}_y\mathrm{H}_z - \mathrm{D}_z\mathrm{H}_y)\,dS$$

$$\frac{d\phi}{ds} = \frac{\partial\phi}{\partial x_\mu}\frac{dx_\mu}{ds}$$

$$\mathbf{F}(\Sigma) = \left(l^2, \frac{l^2}{\beta}, \frac{l^2}{\beta}\right)\mathbf{F}(\Sigma$$

$$\psi = \frac{\partial\phi}{\partial x_\mu}\frac{dx_\mu}{ds}$$

$$\frac{\partial w^\mu}{\partial x_\mu} \equiv \mathfrak{W}^\mu_\mu$$

$$\frac{\partial\mathfrak{W}^\mu_\nu}{\partial x_\mu} - \Gamma^\alpha_{\nu\beta}\mathfrak{W}^\beta_\alpha \equiv \tfrac{1}{2}\mathbf{F}$$

$$\frac{\beta(r'_0 - r')}{lc} = \beta^2\frac{v\xi}{c^2} + \frac{\beta}{lc}\left(\xi\frac{\partial r'}{\partial x} + \eta\frac{\partial r'}{\partial y} + \zeta\frac{\partial r'}{\partial z}\right)$$

$$\mathrm{A}_\mu = \frac{\partial\phi}{\partial x_\mu}$$

$$\frac{^2\gamma_{\mu\nu}}{x_\alpha{}^2} = 2\kappa T^*_{\mu\nu}$$

$$\mathrm{P}_x = \int\rho\xi dS, \quad \mathrm{P}_y = \int\rho\eta dS, \quad \mathrm{P}_z = \int\rho\zeta dS$$

$$\begin{bmatrix}\mu\nu\\\alpha\end{bmatrix} = g_{\alpha\beta}\Gamma^\beta_{\mu\nu}$$

$$\frac{d\mathrm{P}_x}{dt} = \int\rho u_x dS, \quad \frac{d\mathrm{P}_y}{dt} = \int\rho u_y dS, \quad \frac{d\mathrm{P}_z}{dt} = \int\rho u_z$$

$$u_\xi = \frac{u_x - v}{1 - u_x v/c^2}$$

$$u_\eta = \frac{u_y}{\beta(1 - u_x v/c^2)}$$

$$\int K_1 dx_1 dx_2 dx_3 = \int\frac{\partial T_{14}}{\partial x_4}dx_1 dx_2 dx$$

$$u_\zeta = \frac{u_z}{\beta(1 - u_x v/c^2)},$$

$$-i$$

$$\begin{bmatrix}\mu\nu\\\alpha\end{bmatrix} = g_{\alpha\beta}\Gamma^\beta_{\mu\nu}$$

$$\rho' = \frac{\partial\mathrm{X}'}{\partial\xi} + \frac{\partial\mathrm{Y}'}{\partial\eta} + \frac{\partial\mathrm{Z}'}{\partial\zeta}$$

$$= \beta(1 - u_x v/c^2)\rho.$$